PUSHING
AND PULLING

Designed and produced by
Aladdin Books Ltd
PO Box 53987
London SW15 2SF

First published in 2009
by Franklin Watts
338 Euston Road
London NW1 3BH

Franklin Watts Australia
Level 17/207 Kent Street
Sydney NSW 2000

Franklin Watts is a division of Hachette Children's Books,
an Hachette Livre UK company.
www.hachettelivre.co.uk

ISBN 978 0 7496 8633 8

A catalogue record for this book is available from the British Library.

Illustrator: Tony Kenyon

Dewey classification: 531'.11

Printed in Malaysia

Fun Science Projects

PUSHING AND PULLING

GARY GIBSON

ALADDIN / WATTS
London • Sydney

CONTENTS

INTRODUCTION

You have probably tried to walk as a weightless astronaut, and come down to Earth with a bump. Have you stopped to think that there are forces that push and pull us whenever we do anything? With a series of exciting hands-on projects, this book explains some of these fascinating forces, and shows how they work.

ASK AN ADULT TO HELP YOU WITH THIS

Be careful when you are using sharp instruments like scissors – ask an adult to help you.

WHAT IS A FORCE?

If you want to make anything move you have to give it a push or a pull. Scientists call this push or pull a force. Sir Isaac Newton was inspired to write about the force of gravity after an apple landed on his head. The unit of force is called a newton – roughly the force or weight of one apple!

MAKE A FORCE METER

1 Cut out three rectangles from a thick sheet of card. Tape two together to make a 'T'. Tape the third to support the base.

2 Make a small hole near the top of the card. Push through a wooden dowel about 15 centimetres long. Secure firmly.

3 Find a circular-shaped box or tin. Attach two strong threads to the box. Hang the threads from a paper clip.

4 Loop an elastic band through the paper clip. Hang the box from the wooden dowel using the elastic band.

5 Place one object at a time in the box. Note how far the elastic band stretches.

WHY IT WORKS

We can measure how big forces are by seeing how far the elastic band stretches each time. The band must return to its original length after each stretch.

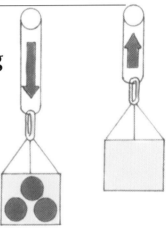

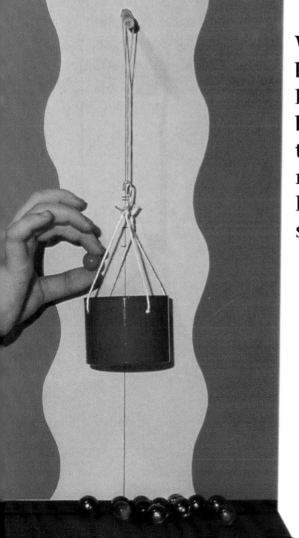

FURTHER IDEAS
Measure the forces made by your own muscles with a set of bathroom scales. Squeeze as hard as you can and check how far the scales go round. Can you push as hard as your own weight?

THE PULL OF GRAVITY

Gravity is the mysterious force: everybody knows it is there but it is very difficult to understand. Planet Earth keeps everything attracted to it quite firmly, because of the pull of gravity. When you see pictures of astronauts floating around in space apparently weightless, they are not being subjected to the Earth's pull of gravity.

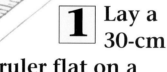

RACE WITH GRAVITY

1 Lay a 30-cm ruler flat on a sheet of white card. Use a pencil to draw a line all around the ruler.

2 Use a pair of scissors to carefully cut out the shape from the card.

3 Divide the card into six equal parts. Colour each part brightly with felt-tip pens.

4 Ask a friend to hold the card hanging down just above your outstretched hand. When your friend releases it, try to catch the card as quickly as you can.

WHY IT WORKS

This is a race between gravity and your body. By the time the message has travelled from your brain to your hand, gravity has pulled  the card down by many centimetres.

FURTHER IDEAS

Ask a friend to drop a small (table tennis) ball down a cardboard tube. Hold a ruler ready near the bottom of the tube. You have to swat the ball before it hits the ground.

BALANCING WEIGHT

We take the art of balance for granted once we have learned to walk as babies. Tightrope walkers have only the thin rope keeping them in the air. Everyone marvels as they balance carefully and defy gravity. This takes great skill as well as courage.

MAKE A BALANCING MAN

1 Draw the 'man' shape onto some thick white card. Carefully cut out the shape with scissors.

2 Colour in the man to make him look more human. Carefully glue a drawing pin to the bottom of the card.

3 Ask an adult to cut off a piece of coat hanger wire. Glue it into place.

4 Make two small plasticine balls of the same size. Wrap one ball around each end of the wire.

5 Carefully stand the balancing man on top of a bottle. He may wobble slightly but should keep his balance.

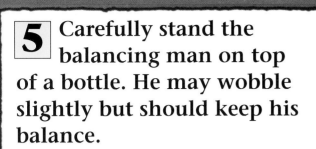

WHY IT WORKS

Gravity keeps everything resting on the ground. In this experiment most of the pulling force of gravity is due to the two heavy balls. It is because these balls are low that the man has a low centre of gravity. Any object will balance when its centre of gravity is low.

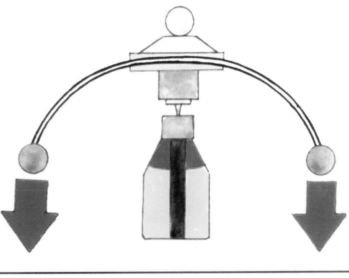

FURTHER IDEAS

You can make a simpler balancing sculpture. Ask an adult to stick a long pin through a cork. Push a fork into each side of the cork. Stand your sculpture on top of a bottle to balance.

SMALL WEIGHTS

You probably see people weighing goods every time you go shopping. They expect to pay for only what they get. 'How much' of something you have is normally measured by its weight. Everything has weight, no matter how small, because of the pull of gravity.

MAKE A MICROBALANCE

1 Cut some thick card into this diamond shape. Fold along the dotted lines.

2 Cut out this shape (slightly over three times the width of a drinking straw) twice from card. Fold into triangular shapes and slide one over each end of a straw.

3 Fold the thick card diamond into a support. Push a steel pin through the card and straw. Strengthen the base with tape.

4 Glue the triangular shape to the ends of the straw. Make sure they balance each other.

5 Remove the front of a cardboard box to screen your microbalance from draughts. Compare the weights of small objects like a pea or bean.

WHY IT WORKS

The heavier an object is, the bigger the force of gravity tugging on it. The side of the straw that is pulled harder will tilt down. When the weights on both sides are equal, then the two forces balance out.

FURTHER IDEAS
Balance a ruler on a pencil. Place an object on each end of the ruler. You can balance two objects of unequal weight by sliding the pencil closer to the lighter object.

FRICTION

Whenever any two things rub against each other, the force of friction tries to stop them. Rubbing your hands together warms them because of friction. Friction is useful because without it there would be no grip! Things would just slip and slide away from each other. Friction can also be a problem because it causes things to overheat.

MEASURING FRICTION

1 Draw the seven shapes A to G on thick card. Carefully cut them out. They will be the parts of your ramp.

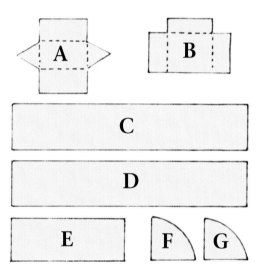

2 Fold shape A along the dotted lines into a prism and stand it on shape C. Tape shape E to shape C. Position shape D between shapes A and E.

3 Fold shape B along the dotted lines into a box. Position it at the end of the ramp. Glue shapes F and G into place. Flip up shape D to make your runway (shape E) steeper.

4 Place a coin at the top of the runway. Slowly make the runway steeper until the coin slides down. Compare with a wooden brick, a rubber and a cork.

WHY IT WORKS

There is more friction, or grip, between rough surfaces than between smooth ones. Even though the rubber and the card feel smooth, they have tiny rough edges. Only when the runway is steep enough, can this grip between rubber and card be overcome.

FURTHER IDEAS

Cut out a piece of aluminium foil to fit your runway. Carefully lay it flat and into place. Repeat your tests. Is there more friction from the aluminium compared to the card? Compare other surfaces, such as felt, plastic or paper. Can you tell which surface has the most friction?

GETTING A GRIP

Grip is very important to drivers. The wheels of a vehicle can slide, especially on slippery surfaces like mud, and may cause an accident. Tractors' wheels are very big and knobbly to increase their grip on muddy fields.

MAKE A COTTON REEL TRACTOR

1 Ask an adult to cut off a disc from the end of a candle and to remove the wick.

2 Cut out two circles of card to fit the ends of a cotton reel. Make a small hole in the centre and tape each into place.

3 Thread a small elastic band through the wax disc. Stop it from going all the way through by looping the end around a matchstick.

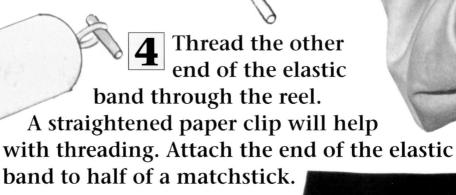

4 Thread the other end of the elastic band through the reel. A straightened paper clip will help with threading. Attach the end of the elastic band to half of a matchstick.

5 Wind up the big matchstick tightly without breaking the elastic band. Place the tractor on the floor, and let the matchstick push it along.

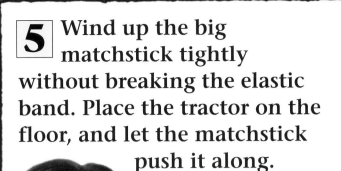

WHY IT WORKS

The wound up elastic band stores energy. As the elastic band starts to unwind, it makes the big matchstick rotate. The matchstick presses against the ground. Since one end of the matchstick cannot move against the ground, the energy is used up by making the cotton reel rotate instead. This is what pushes the tractor forwards.

FURTHER IDEAS
Wrap elastic bands around the reel to act as rubber tyres and improve the grip. See what is the steepest slope it can climb up. (Use the friction tester on pages 14 and 15).

HYDRAULIC FORCES

Powerful machines like cranes, fork-lift trucks and fire engines use hydraulic forces to lift heavy things quite easily. 'Hydro' means water, although in practice these machines use other liquids in their hydraulics.

MAKE A HYDRAULIC FORCE

1 Ask an adult to cut the necks off two large plastic bottles. Then to cut a hole near the bottom of each.

2 Thread a plastic tube through the bottles. Tie the neck of a balloon over one end of the tube. Fill the other end with water.

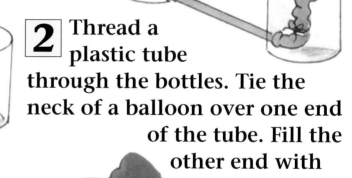

3 Fill another balloon with water. Tie this balloon to the free end of the tube. Both balloons and the tube must be filled with water.

4 Find two empty tins that just fit into the bottles. Place them above the balloons. Gently push down on one tin with the palm of your hand.

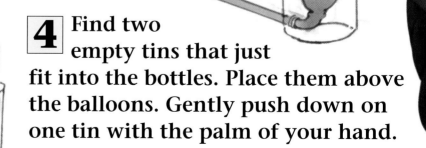

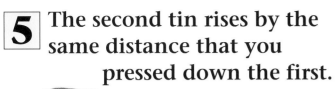

5 The second tin rises by the same distance that you pressed down the first. You can reverse this by pressing down on the second tin.

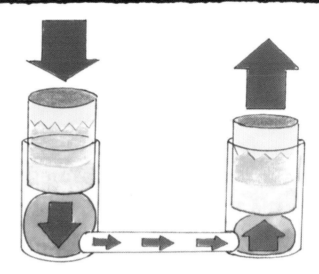

WHY IT WORKS

It is very difficult to squash water. If you squeeze it hard in one place, it will push out just as hard in another place. The water transmits the force from one tin to the other. This is the principle used by all hydraulic machines.

FURTHER IDEAS

Glue a small plastic toy to a balloon. Connect the balloon to a plastic syringe with a tube. Lay the balloon flat in a glass tumbler and inflate with the syringe. This pump uses air, which is springy compared to water, to make the balloon inflate.

WHAT A DRAG!

It is quite hard to move quickly under the water. The water gets in your way and before you can move forward you must push it out of the way. The water exerts a special force of friction called 'drag'. Birds and aeroplanes have wings designed to reduce 'drag' in the air.

TESTING MOVING SHAPES

1 Find a large plastic bottle and ask an adult to cut off the neck. Otherwise use a long plastic tube.

2 Find a small but sturdy box. Cut a piece of thick card and tape it to the back of the box.

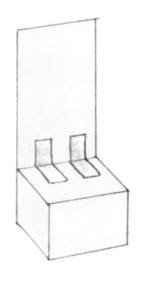

3 Use a funnel to carefully fill the bottle with cooking oil. Stand the bottle on the box.

4 Mould the same amount of plasticine into different shapes. Attach a piece of cotton to each shape.

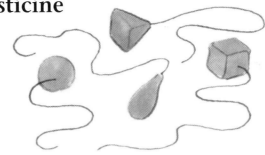

5 Hold the shapes just above the bottle, release and start timing. Make sure you hold on to the cotton. Stop timing when the shapes reach the bottom.

WHY IT WORKS

Cooking oil has more drag than water so it is easier to see how much the shapes are slowed down. A shape has to push the oil out of its path to move forwards. Shapes with a rounded front allow liquids to pass around them with little drag.

FURTHER IDEAS

Try some of these shapes. Predict which will move the fastest before you test them. Add a small weight to the front of each shape to stop it from turning around as it falls.

PULLEYS

A pulley is a machine to help you lift very heavy loads. Cranes are useful machines with a system of pulleys that make lifting heavy objects easier. You can see cranes almost everywhere – on building sites, at docks and at railway stations.

MAKE A SIMPLE PULLEY

1 Cut out a window from some card. Fold it and tape a triangle to the back to help it stand up. Push a short wooden dowel through the top.

2 Cut 4 circles of card, each with a hole in the middle. Push a piece of straw through each pair of circles.

3 Bend three pieces of thin wire into shape. Attach the circles to the wire to make one double pulley and one single pulley.

4 Hang the pulleys as shown. Make sure you loop the string around the lower pulley, back over the top pulley and out through the window.

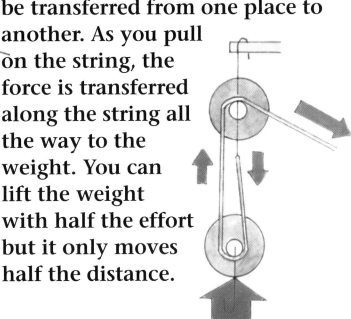

WHY IT WORKS

A pulley system allows a force to be transferred from one place to another. As you pull on the string, the force is transferred along the string all the way to the weight. You can lift the weight with half the effort but it only moves half the distance.

5 Hang a small weight from the hook on the lower pulley. Pull the string from behind the window to lift the weight.

FURTHER IDEAS
Make a winch from a card base and plasticine-filled straw. Hold the straw in place with wire. Wrap string around the straw, and tie a hook to the other end. Attach weights to the hook and pull them in by winding the winch.

AROUND AND AROUND

Electric mixers, washing machines and dryers all operate by spinning forces. A gyroscope is a terrific toy that seems to defy gravity while it spins. The spinning force balances out the force of gravity and makes the spinning object hard to push over.

MAKE SPINNING TOPS

1 Find a large sheet of thin white card. Use a pair of compasses to draw some circles of different sizes.

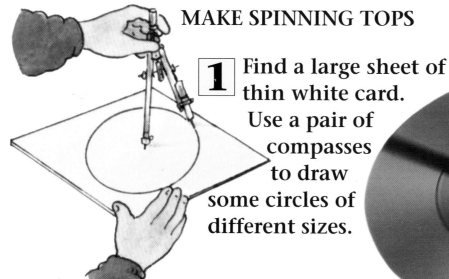

2 Use a pair of scissors to cut out each circle carefully.

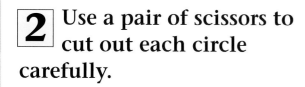

3 Colour each circle with bright markers. Create a different design for each one.

4 Make a small hole through the centre of each circle. Then push a sharp pencil through each hole.

WHY IT WORKS

When you start the top spinning, you give it a lot of spinning energy. The top spins for minutes before this energy is all used up. The top actually stores some of the energy during this time so that it can go on spinning. The energy you gave it is only gradually released.

5 Hold the top of the pencil between two fingers and spin it as fast as you can. Release it and let it spin on a smooth table top.

FURTHER IDEAS
Place an egg on a plate and start it spinning fast. Suddenly grab the egg to stop it spinning. Quickly release it and it will start spinning again all by itself!

TRANSFERRING FORCES

All of the power in a modern car comes from the engine. The forces made by the engine are then transferred to where they are needed – mainly to make the wheels turn. One of the most common ways of transferring forces is through gear wheels.

MAKE A MODEL CAR

1 Draw and cut out four equal circles with teeth all the way around them using thick card. These are your gear wheels.

2 Make a small hole in the middle of each wheel. Add another close to the middle of one wheel. Draw and cut out the other shapes shown here.

3 Use a paper clip to attach one wheel to a piece of card. Insert an extra piece of card between the card and paper clip for a tight fit.

4 Attach the other wheel to the bar and hammer with a paper clip. Attach these to the first wheel so that the teeth match.

5 Rotate the upper wheel slowly. Watch how the hammer moves from side to side.

WHY IT WORKS

As you turn the first gear wheel, this turning movement is passed on to the second gear wheel. The bar moves from side to side as the wheel turns and this sets up the sideways movement of the hammer.

FURTHER IDEAS

Try using different-sized wheels in your gear system. Notice how they move at different speeds. The larger gears move more slowly than the smaller gears.

EQUAL AND OPPOSITE

Forces always come in pairs. When a cannon fires a shell, the cannon itself recoils. The force pushing the shell FORWARDS has an equal but opposite force.

MAKE A JET ENGINE

1 Cut out these shapes from thin card. Tape the strip into a circle. Attach a drinking straw.

2 Tape together all of the shapes to make up the outline of a rocket like the one illustrated below.

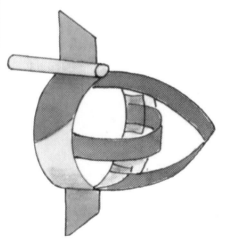

3 Place a balloon in the card. Slowly inflate it until it is a tight fit inside the rocket outline. Keep holding the neck of the balloon.

4 Thread string through the straw. Fasten the ends of the string across the room. Release the balloon to be jet-propelled along the string.

WHY IT WORKS

Over 300 years ago, Sir Isaac Newton found that every force has an equal but opposite reaction. As the air rushes out of the back of your balloon in one direction, the balloon itself is pushed forwards in the opposite direction. This is the principle on which all jet engines work.

FURTHER IDEAS
Sit in a chair with wheels, and hold a football. Try to throw it without moving. The harder you throw it, the stronger the opposite force is that pushes you backwards.

FANTASTIC FORCE FACTS

The famous Italian scientist Galileo (1564–1642) studied gravity by watching the way things fall. His experiments included throwing stones from the top of the Leaning Tower of Pisa.

The British scientist Sir Isaac Newton (1642–1727), was able to describe how the force of gravity makes things fall after being hit on the head by a falling apple.

The Saturn V rocket pushes with a force equivalent to the combined power of 30 diesel train engines.

Meteorites rarely hit Earth. When they hit the Earth's atmosphere at high speed, there is friction between the air and the meteorites. This causes them to burn up.

Rockets and space shuttles break through the Earth's gravitational pull. To do so they must reach speeds of 40,000 kilometres per hour.

The heaviest load ever lifted was the offshore Ekofisk complex in the North Sea. The complex weighed 44,000 tonnes and was lifted 6.5 metres by 122 hydraulic jacks.

The brakes on a Formula One racing car glow red. This is caused by the friction of the disc pads on the discs.

The longest time anyone has balanced on a tightrope is 205 days. Jorge Ojeda-Guzman of Orlando, Florida, stunned crowds by walking, balancing on a chair and dancing on a wire 11 metres long.

The largest tyres manufactured were by Goodyear Tire and Rubber Co. for giant dumper trucks. They were 3.6 metres in diameter and weighed 5,670 kg (12,500 lb).

The longest recorded pull in a tug of war is 24 minutes, 45 seconds between Ireland and England during the Tug of War World Championships, in 1988.

GLOSSARY

Drag
The resistance of air or water. A force that holds back moving objects.

Energy
When a force moves an object, energy is passed to the object (where it may be saved). This is called work. Heat, light and power are forms of energy.

Force
A push, pull or twist that makes an object move or change direction. For example, throwing a ball is exerting force on the ball which makes it move.

Friction
A force occurs when two surfaces rub against each other. It always slows movement, and brings motion to a stop if no other force is applied to overcome it.

Gravity
The pulling force of the Earth that makes things fall and gives things weight.

Grip
The action of a surface on another as a result of friction.

Gyroscope
A spinning top that stays upright even if its supports are moved.

Hydraulics
The use of liquids, particularly water, in engineering. Hydraulic systems are used for transmitting energy.

Lift
An upward force acting on wings or fins of animals, or the wings of an aeroplane.

Power
The rate at which energy is changed from one form to another. The power of moving car engines is measured in brake horsepower (bhp).

Pulley
A system of wheels and rope that allows heavy loads to be lifted more easily.

INDEX